I0416498

# Panola: My Kinfolks' Land

## By

## Evelyn Dilworth-Williams

This book is a work of fiction. Places, events, and situations in this story are purely fictional. Any resemblance to actual persons, living or dead, is coincidental.

© 2002 by Evelyn Dilworth-Williams. All rights reserved.

No part of this book may be reproduced, stored in a retrieval system, or transmitted by any means, electronic, mechanical, photocopying, recording, or otherwise, without written permission from the author.

ISBN: 1-4033-8201-8 (e-book)
ISBN: 1-4033-8202-6 (Paperback)

This book is printed on acid free paper.

1stBooks – rev. 01/13/03

# *Acknowledgements*

Panola, a milieu of pleasurable memories laced with an awe-inspiring people, as beautiful as a non-clouded sunrise on a brisk autumn morning. The people of this terra firma yield the spirit of my poetry that I've harvested for life.

The splendor of the poetic written word
Becomes the reality of non-presence but yet heard
Poetry is the conveyance of my feeling for living
To be shared beyond the bodily appearance of giving
Poetry is the emblematic vehicle of my communication
Imparted with love to all in human creation
In hopes that reading it will inspire a daily breath
To tap the emotions beyond the surface depth
May the words on these printed pages that are read
Weave a harmonious human tapestry with poetic thread

Special thanks to Thomas my husband, Chris and Jeff my sons, and LaTrease my daughter-in-law, for all of their support, as well as their patience with me as I would so anxiously await for the right moment to share my poetry.

Thanks to all my siblings, and their families for the encouragement they always gave to me about every poem I've shared with them. An extraordinary thanks to my six sisters: Claudia, Ruby, Minerva, Peggy, Ann, and Delois for always loving all that I wrote, and saying inspiring words to me. To my three brothers: Guy, James and Charles for the special comments they always made about my poetry. Thanks to my Aunt Brat (Susan Carmichael), for accepting my poems as something to treasure.

Thanks to my Sunday school members and mission sisters for their support and love. A heartfelt thanks to my pastor, Reverend Samuel Pettegrue, for the many moving sermons that enthused me to write so many of my poems, and to his wife Beverly for being such a wonderful first lady of Sardis Baptist Church. I also want to thank the rest of my church family at Sardis Baptist Church for their special encouragement.

Thanks to my coworkers and beautiful students at Holy Family High School for the positive responses they gave when they read my poems.

I would be remiss if I didn't thank Vanessa Davis Griggs for sharing her infinite knowledge about writing and publishing.

Thanks to my life long friends who always define my poems as something special to them.

Last but not least, thanks to my childhood friend, Lil' Velma, for her kind and inspiring words about my poetry.

This book of poetry is dedicated in memory of my parents Guy and Bertha Louise Dilworth, and in memory of my maternal and paternal grandparents, Flenoy and Ruby Little (Cuzin Boosey & Sis Ruby), and Cleve and Minerva Dilworth.

# Table of Contents

Let the words of my mouth, and the meditation of my heart, be acceptable in thy sight, O Lord, my strength, and my redeemer.

*Psalm* 19: 14

# Blackland Prairie

**A land of dark colored surface layers and yellowish colored subsoil intermingled with home grounded values and memories.**

*Evelyn Dilworth-Williams*

# My Evening Song

Whether I'm There or Not!

Rose early this morning with a full day ahead
All sorts of thoughts runnin' through my head
Stopped to praise Him for allowing me to get out of bed
Filling me with the spirit to tackle life's daily dreads.

Interactin' with my love ones and feelin' so wondrously blessed
Hardly could restrain myself from shoutin' while gettin' dressed
Knowin' this time was an accurate measurement of no space for jest
I just praised Him for giving me a new day after a good night's rest.

The day unfolded without any effort on my part
While half started preparing for tomorrow's start
Rushin' to make do of time left as if it would never restart
Overwrought my mind stiflin' good choices I needed to impart.

Runnin' frantically on half empty and with lots of things left to do
Made me mindful of tomorrow and that each day was brand new
Settlin' my mind that part of today is what tomorrow will pursue
And the forthcoming of each day will relentlessly continue.

Whether I'm There Or Not!
so I'll just sing songs of praise …
never in doubt of His power,
not even amazed.

# Watching Wonders

A snowflake resting on a daffodil,
Seems unlikely yet it's real,
Wondering what's next to be revealed,
Still watching a snowflake on a daffodil.

Mysteries come and never disappear,
Can't grasp the origin so we stand in fear,
Time is presented with the Savior so near,
Hopeful that the mysteries will never disappear.

Just a snowflake on a daffodil,
Makes for understanding to disappear.
Still the promise of the Savior is near,
With a snowflake resting on a daffodil.

# Baby Raising

A baby is born
and we gather
or maybe not
yet
someone is in need
of the rules
to the game
of life
starting and finishing
is the task
to get the baby
through stages
of
the game of life
who will it be
me, you, or someone else
perchance the world itself
someone got a job to do
who's up for the task
me, you, or someone else
maybe
the
baby.

# Mrs. Mae Lou's Business

There was a woman in my neighborhood that washed everyday,
She hung her clothes a peculiar kind of way.
Her wash was hung around the same time of day,
The clothes looked so bad from the dingy wash, wear, and play.
I noticed at home she always stayed,
Her name was Mrs. Mae Lou from across the way.

I often wanted to tell her to re-wash what she had hung,
But as she washed she seemed so happy singing those ole timey songs,
I guess her eyes were not what they used to be when she was young,
A sigh of relief she gave when that ole dingy wash was hung.
Mrs. Mae Lou puzzled me why she never got her wash clean,
I started to tell her but her friendship I felt might wean.

I invited my neighbor in to see what I was talking about,
Looked through my window and claimed she couldn't see out.
She strained her eyes but she couldn't see what I was trying to show,
So I stopped and washed my window so it would glow.
Mrs. Mae Lou's wash was cleaner than anyone could know.

To my amazement it was not Mrs. Mae Lou's wash that was unclean,
But my own dirt on my window that made me see what I had seen.
'Cause Mrs. Mae Lou's wash was like a bright sparkling sheen.
Now rarely do I look at anyone's wash on his or her clothesline,
My time is spent cleaning all my windows of dirt that's mine.

# Mama's Morning

Mama rises so early each day,
Begins in a hurry, but doesn't forget to pray.
She starts kneading bread in a bowl of hope,
Sun rays appear to reassure peace so she can cope.

Busy preparing the meal to master her love ones daily pace,
She knows her strength comes only from abundant grace.
She lovingly stirs all kinds of tolerance and contentment,
That renders spiritual sustenance not worldly resentment.

She blends all types of courage for each love one,
Being very careful to leave out none.
Making sure there's an extra helping of family peace,
Mama softly prays and never ceases.

She loudly calls everyone to the table to eat,
Mama's in a hurry there's a clock to beat.
The bowls placed before all are so very deep,
She wants none of her meal to overflow, but to keep.

With stern gentility she encourages all to take in enough,
For daily spiritual nourishment digests life that's rough.
Mama smiles as her family dines,
Knowing they are in the hands of no earthly kind.

Now the bowls are finally cleaned,
Mama is still smiling for she knows what that means.
Doors start to swing open as all departs,
And Mama smiles again and puts her hand over her heart.

"See you later," she would always say,
If you look back you could see and hear her pray.
Mama is so pleased with the riches of His glory,
For when properly fed her love ones will live to tell His story.

# Never Alone

My shadow is there whether day or night
When darkness causes doubt I just step into the light
For my shadow is there both day and night
Sometimes forgetting His presence is always near
I'll just stand in the light and my shadow will appear
My shadow stands by me in spite of earthly fear

Whether darkness or light,
My shadow keeps me in sight.

When in doubt I just step into the light
For my shadow is there both day and night
Never alone even when time increases its pace
My shadow is the Master's heavenly grace
I follow my shadow from day to night
My shadow keeps me in His heavenly sight
When darkness causes me doubt I just step into the light
For my shadow is there both day and night.

# Sisters

Six in one hand or half a dozen in the other,
This number doesn't include my three brothers.
So much alike in presence and thought,
The design of the other one is often caught.
The sharing of bruises from our souls,
A commonplace in our life's stories told.
The beauty of our essence is a mixture from all,
Yet separate we know how to conquer life's call.
The definition of our being sometimes appears weak,
But constant hands of assurance are always there to seek.
There is an understanding of any slip up that appear,
For none is absent when the other got a tear.
A constant intermingling with the life of the other,
Yet always seeking the presence of the three brothers.
The spirit of unity that surrounds the heart of each one,
Gives a certainty of life's comfort and denied to none.
When the need to adjust one of life's plan,
A bond of energy sharing takes command.
The potency of the totality of numbers,
Carries a spirit to lessen life's blunders.
Abiding in the belief of the power to pray,
Places an eternal seal of sister bond to stay.
Each one unique in the pattern of life's kind,
Yet heavily stroked with likeness from the hands of Thine.
All are spun from the sameness granted to the three brothers,
And all six are very much like our father and mother.
Six, three, and I make for the family's yield,
And each adds a portion that makes the family real.
Six in one hand or half a dozen in the other,
And this number doesn't include my three brothers.

# I Know Her

Walking along at a steady pace
Smiling at all in the human race
Arms and hands crossed behind her back
Studyin' how to keep life on track.

Greatness is revealed in her face
Never wondering who is her savior and grace
Showing strength in all of her endeavors
Knowing all that she does must be clever.

Making sure no one is ever slighted
Seeking answers for all not so delighted
Leaning on wisdom beyond all man
Not caring how others view her stand.

Protecting all of hers with loyalty and pride
Never wondering who is always by her side
Walking along at a steady pace
Appreciate her, she bears the human race.

# Woman's Work Is Never Done

The carrier of life's treasures lies in the belly of man's help meet,
Bringing forth seeds of life to never retreat.
To nurture from conception until death's conquest,
Her touch is soft, yet firm enough to settle and stir unrest.

The power to carry the seeds of humanity is a job never done,
She prepares for being's existence as long as there is a rise in the sun.
The sustaining and the clinging of life's seeds,
Keep the design of her in touch with all that humanity needs.

Her earthly statue is a vision of what is small,
Yet she prepares to make and keep safety of the universe's all.
She is sometimes tired and sometimes weary,
But when the seeds of humanity are threatened beware of her fury.

The design of the world is the platform of her workplace,
So she molds and shapes it to assure certainty of the human race.
The task before her is of a great challenge,
With an inborn spirit of surviving she is balanced.

Her work is constantly in some stage of manifestation,
Still ready is she for all of the Master's creation.

# Lil' Lizzie

From head to toe small in size of visible statue,
Yet her presence commands a grandeur reaction.
Strutting with her head upright as she clicks her heels,
Smiling so big that her inner spirit is revealed.

Hardly ever getting where she's supposed to be,
For she stops and speaks to everybody she sees.
She takes inventory of all those in need,
Giving her diminutive substance to share and feed.

All that she does she never wants told,
Yet it's tucked away in hearts to forever hold.
Kind and encouraging words always embrace her being,
And it removes despair to make way for recovering.

She injects a spirited laugh that upgrades everybody's smile,
For it comes from the inner soul of the Master's child.
Little in statue but big in heart,
Her love for humanity will never depart.

# My Sisters' Baby Brother

Born to be outnumbered by the opposite gender,
Yet destined to play the role as their defender.
Caring for others is a commonplace task,
Never to dodge behind an assigned mask.

Engulfed with the energy to assure all is well,
Tends to befit his being wherever he dwells.
Receptive of others with some of life's diminishes,
And will give support until all is well or finished.

Spun with the tendency to conquer life's defeats,
Recognizes the energy that continues life's entreats.
Sometimes withdrawn yet always ready to do his part,
For his energy is sent straight from his heart.

The inner power of his being is to protect,
And does it well for none does he neglect.
His effort to upgrade a heart that's skipping a beat,
Magnifies his concern of others he meet.

Caught in the middle of so many females,
Tendered his maleness but male prowess never frail.
With the look of his father and none other,
And the spirit of willingness to give from his mother,
Shows face for my childhood playmate, my baby brother.

# There's More

There's a big road in the far off distance
Yet I travel the one with the least resistance
Routinely familiarity makes my day
The burden of no growth fills me with dismay
Still out in the distance I see the big road
And dream of letting it handle my life's loads.

# Narcissistic Me

I'm going to keep my eyes on me today,
I'll listen closely to what I will say.
To widely view all of my integrated interactions,
Affords me all that's needed for peaceful reactions.
Harnessing my view will clearly soften the tone,
Of my spirit that will surface and be shown.
I'll just look at me as the day continues to pass,
Then for sure I'll notice what is needed to last.
My eyes will watch carefully only me,
And faults in others I will not see.
To concentrate on what my day will hold,
Will diminish the idea of others to control.
To watch me will help fix all that I need,
And deny me pain of other people's greed.
The task to watch me will not be with ease,
For I'm a difficult one for me to please.
As the day graduate to a guaranteed close,
Thoughts will wonder what did I really expose.
I'll wean myself from an interpreted vision of another,
'Cause looking at me deflects intolerance of all others.

# Sassy Me

I can't shine your shoes and tap dance too,
Too much of that makes me blue.
My problems are not there when I chew and walk,
It's the noise from your direction when you bellow and balk.

Sitting renders such great daily pleasure,
It only ceases when you attempt my life's measure.
Laughing loud is such good medicine to my soul,
So keep what you say and never speak until you are told.

Worry me not about how it should be,
Inasmuch as that makes me not show you what you attempt to see.
Crying is all right too, but just for a short while,
Don't confuse yourself thinking that is how I walk my mile.

I enjoy everything possible that I can do,
So don't dictate my standards just take care of you.
Demands on me can no longer come from your voice,
You can only react to me based on my choice.

Don't think that my life will be spent sufficing your needs,
'Cause my life is sustained not by yours but by the Master and my
deeds.

# Show Pony: PHASE I

no mo donkeying in life
and I taint talkin' basketball
just cain't haul this load no mo
my back has been soothingly scratched
by hands from a non-despairing batch

show ponying is my remaining life's role
strutting onto the pavement for the bold
heads turning from side to side
watchin' only the direction of my peace
to exist for the days of smiles to keep

changed myself from head to toe
yet the ole multi-mule is forever there
just stifled 'til self-assurance takes hold
to pristinely show what renders a trot
that reveals my needed self-assigned lot

from a donkey
to a mule
and a mule
to a show pony
which is most beneficial
to be
just watch the absent domestic ass
to see

# Panola

The morning air caresses my being with a tantalizing hold,
Magically stirring my day to a wondrous story to be told.
The agrarian perfumed air fills me with a natural brew,
And all that I grasp is old but emerges as brand new.

An over joy of energy springs forth to embark,
Staying with my presence until my view is dark.
Anointed by nature's gift of country life,
Interlocks my soul with all that's void of strife.

My vision is enhanced by a canopy of green fields,
That is dampened with the morning dew as its shield.
Then sun rays blaze and fall where growth is instilled,
Grasping what's needed for an increase to be revealed.

Astonished at the work of such a planned show,
Embraced my outlook of the day as nature grows.
Mesmerized by the statue of those who daily toiled,
With a constant display of love as they tilled the soil.

My soul is ingrained into this peaceful place,
As I breathe the country air as a gift from grace.
Precious is this moment of my assigned time to share,
A place that was given by those who toiled with care.

As the toilers laid their tools down for an endless rest,
It's on this site that my soul breathes to harvest my best.
For what was planted by those before me will forever stand,
On this rural countryside called Panola, my kinfolks' land.

# The Oak and Me

That ole oak tree planted so long ago
Withered in spots and continues to grow
Still it spreads and stands pristinely tall
And can make shade for nature's all

Hewing it down would be such a waste
Nature will grow another with haste
As the limbs age through time's course
The ole oak just towers with no remorse

Seemingly it stands longer than most can stay
Providing shade to anyone who passes its way
Time is detected by the visibility of its bark
Still serenaded when perched by a meadowlark

Just a tree that breathes longer than me
Planted by nature for everyone to see
Its wear is slow as it bows through time
Standing there to forever rise over mankind

Just a tree that breathes longer than me.

# The Path and the Big Road

The path I travel is a thorny one to me,
For it's blinding with life's prickly debris.
Still I travel it though I can't see,
This path just won't let me walk free.

I'm forever bending to miss a stick,
The flair to dodge is not my time-vested trick.
I blink my eyes and miss my directions,
The path gets void of my life's connections.

Mystically I can see an adjoining big road,
But it's a hard path-link because of life's load.
Traveling seems set from beginning to end,
The path gets narrow yet I can walk if I pretend.

Still the adjoining road never leaves my sight,
It follows like the sun from morning 'til night.
Maybe I'll veer to see what's up the big road,
But surely I'll carry some of life's load.

The switch from the path is a welcomed change,
The big road takes my load to quickly rearrange.
Now I walk in the middle of the big road; and comfort I feel,
Still there's left-right room in the big road for a path that's genteel.

Walking now I see with a clear view,
Everything in sight seems so deservingly new.
Life's travels are in tune with what's needed to pursue,
Created by the Divine, not just for me but you too.

# The Plowman

The morning day starts with the rise of the sun
Shining on barren fields that can't be shunned
The plowman swings open the stable gate
Making ready for rows to be made straight.

The reign hangs in its usual place
Against the wall in its own space
Awaiting someone to use it for control
To reap the rewards for life to behold.

Off in the distant a helper is in sight
Standing ready for use of his inborn might
The reign and helper embrace for the day
To be used by the plowman as he may.

The morning rows need great concentration
And firm holding makes for needed application
While plowing directly into the harden terrain
The bridled helper yields to the command of the reign.

The day wears with the sun's hottest beams
The difficulty of straight rows eases as it seems
The reign loosens as the helper gives way to the task
For the plowman had little of the helper to ask.

The morning field to the evening field
Had a change in an outward show to reveal
All rows were perfectly aligned in the same way
The need to not rein in was at the end of the day.

Between the rising and the setting of the sun
The reign and the helper meshed into one
As the plowman's hold slackens throughout the day
Unbending rows were made by the helper as he may.

# O' Sinner Man

Like a fallen leaf separating from a tree,
Without anchor in parts of Thee.
My essence no longer carries God in my heart,
I've decide to make for a different start.

Vibrant and steadfast as I used to be,
Living in the world has replaced Thee.
Can't seem to find my blessed way,
For in this dwelling I can't find time to pray.

Amazing as your wonders have always been,
Can't seem to see them for this obstruction of sin.
Yet freedom to worship I hear is still around,
Can't find churches on this side of town.

Living this way makes for such worldly fun,
People of all types but no believers in His Son.
Looking around in search of a familiar face,
Getting close to find they are not in this place.

Oh how different it used to be,
With the stretch of my hand toward Thee.
Remembering never stays with me long,
For my life is submerged in appetizing wrong.

Times are different as I travel this way,
Still there's something within that always say:
O' sinner man, sinner man, just stretch out your hand,
Before your birth you were part of His plan.

No longer are you needed to carry the weight of sin,
For when He hung His head and died that came to an end.
O' sinner man, sin no more,
Quietly stand and you'll hear Him knock on the door.

He's there to free you of all sin,
No matter how wretched you've been.
His love cleanses from beginning to end,
Just open the door and let Him in.

# That Ole Shack

There was an ole broken down shack,
Standing adjacent to ole noisy drift track,
Ne'er understood why people would leave and come back,
Everything seemed in disarray but no one would react.

Somethin' seemed not right in that ole shack,
That appeared to have less than ordinary tact,
Still people came out looking so relaxed,
As if they had proof of some supernatural act.

Then one day out came a line of mourners,
Taking something around the corner,
Gently putting it away and left it as a loner,
And looking as if they would too be a joiner.

But slowly they returned to that ole shack,
That stands adjacent to drift track,
So I got in line and went and sat in the back,
Up front was readin' from a book that was black.

Everyone sat and listened to the Word,
Thank you Lord, is what I heard,
Someone said, "Father, Son and the Holy Ghost is third,"
That's when I knew I could do more than stand by and observe.
So I kneeled and humbly prayed; now I too can be heard.

That ole shack doesn't seem so ole to me anymore,
'Cause I'm lookin' from the inside like the others before,
Oh what an amazing place to be,
That I do not judge what I can not see.

# Sunday Dinner

A day of chicken and dumplings served on a pretty plate,
Everybody came to the table and nobody was late.
Heads bowed and thanked the Almighty for what was done,
Eager to eat, talk and quiet was none.

The heartfelt glances around the room,
Eased all pain from previous days of gloom.
Everybody got full, not just from the meal,
But from the surrender of love the family revealed.

The rhythmic sound of the forks and spoons,
Mixed with laughter came to an end too soon.
The table was cleaned of its plentiful blessings,
Yet the family remained seated sharing and confessing.

What the meal's bounty could not fill in the family's soul,
An added portion of God's Word came from the young and old.
The intake balanced itself with flavor and the Word,
That's when Sunday dinner was completely served.

# Family Reunion

Coming together with smiles on our faces,
Hugging and kissing then stopping to tie shoe laces.

Walking and talking about the old and new,
Everybody's happy; thank God no one's blue.

Grinning and laughing with each other aloud,
Never caring about the stares from a distant crowd.

Sharing the joys along with the aches and pains,
But feelings of gladness that everyone came.

Stroking the little ones as they run and play,
Yet tearing-up now and then as we pray.

Missing the love ones who have gone to their eternal home,
Knowing the presence of their spirit never leaves us alone.

Still smiling and chuckling throughout our stay,
Lord, we're so glad you made this family reunion day.

# The Family's Garden

Here is the family's garden with all sorts of plants,
All standing tall not even the little ones will slant.
The roots are so similar with such an unyielding hold,
For all have received enough rays that make them bold.

The garden is so beautiful with its striking array,
All the plants are nourished by time taken to pray.
An abundance of living water is in constant flow,
For it's the sure way the family plants will grow.

Sometimes the rushing wind causes the plants to lose tact,
But the roots are so strong that they just bounce back.
Barrels of bushel love are always reaped,
The family plants stay grounded to forever keep.

When a storm maker bows the plants to the ground,
They unbend 'cause the root creator is always around.
Such a heavenly fixed garden down here on earth,
That is blessed with supported roots from birth.

Showers from family tears pour to help the plants grow,
That's the gift that makes the family plants adornment show.
The family garden never loses the beauty of its sight,
The caretaker works from morning through the night.

Blessed are we to grow in the family garden's lot,
Sustained from the roots that are protected by the Master's plot.
Just a blessed garden strengthened by family ties from above,
Ne'er to change because of heavenly ordained sent love.

# Day of Rain

Just wearing the warmth of rain
Enjoying life absence of strain
Then:
Gazing at the blossoms of spring
Looking forward to what life will bring
Now:
Stepping on the saturated ground
While hearing the rain come down
And:
Snuggling to the mist in the air
Wondering if anyone else is really there
Yet:
So consciously loving the steady sound
From the touches of the rain from all around
While:
Prophetically enjoying all that I've gain
Still happily embracing the pouring rain.

*Evelyn Dilworth-Williams*

# Needs Fulfilled

Order my pace,
With your loving grace.
Starve the inner enemy of earthly hate,
With your eternally blessed fate.

Reshuffle my dreams with reality's measure,
Your will is the only real mindful treasure.
While filling my days with worthy hope,
Your view of life is a precious scope.

Guide my love ones with your hallowed light,
Binding them with your protective might.
Still letting me enjoy the birds as they sing,
Such heavenly creatures this life brings.

Show your celestial stars night after night,
The beauty they give is sacred in my sight.
Rest my soul to embrace the moon while alone,
That is the splendor which soothes my bones.

Laughter I need to balance life's contrition,
Universal energy comes without my commission.
Spare me from harm that lurks around,
You shield so well I'm always astounded.

Your hand is something I'll always need,
Guaranteed guidance is there before I plea.
Oh how precious is your being,
Faithfulness I promise you without seeing.

Sort my thoughts of days of uncertainty,
For your will is my unconscious veracity.
Shelter my life's trust of eternal peace,
Securing me blessings that will not cease.

# Peace

The reality of my truth is His guiding light
Staying intact with honesty about heaven's sight
Rendering the gift of justice to all His saints
Keeps me strong never weary nor faint.

Enabling the heart's purity to become my thoughts
With lovely signals to annul evil's value to naught
And that of good report my soul will embrace
These gift come by way of His abundant grace.

'Cause no man renders the heart's need of nurture
The God of Abraham gives all these virtues
Peace I'll forever make with Him
Keeping life's light from growing dim.

# Reaping

The most that we can receive is what we give,
Life returns spring forth on how we live.
An abundance of sufficient means,
Depends on reality, not just dreams.

The gift of giving is the ultimate prize,
Life becomes meaningful once that's realized.
The denial of what makes a day worthwhile,
Comes from not sharing with the Master's child.

To receive and not share your portion,
Tends to render an infectious earthly motion.
Grace allows the gathering of what one needs.
So give what you get, for the wise will take heed.

# Yielding

The imposing presence of a mountain's height,
Reveals the impotence of man's might.
Squandering below the colossal formation,
Extracts from reality the minuteness of His creation.

A mountain that mutters not a single word,
Yet in its presence the finiteness of man is heard.
Standing at the foothill and never seeing the peak,
Is not the image man can valiantly keep.

This giant configuration in the presence of man,
Is divinely designed to gauge who is grand.
Our efforts are to challenge what's greater than you and me,
So we mastermind a climb to set our self-bated nature free.

The mountain stands motionless as we attempt our massive win,
Even when we reach the top the slopes down won't give in.
The mountain never bows to man's desire to explore,
Nor yielding to us at the top or at the foothills as before.

The mountain majestically claims its assigned stand,
To remind us of our place in life's enormous plan.
To share a world with something bigger than man,
Edifies the mountain to reveal what is God-made grand.

Something is greater than you and me,
Whether we challenge it so we can see.
Sill something is greater than you and me.
*Rising above our essence into the sky
* For He rose above our essence beyond the sky.

* interchangeable lines

# Lonely Love

My being tucks away my lonely love,
It stays in place like a peaceful dove.

Deep in the corners of my soul,
Lonely love stays silent, as I grow old.

Penetrated into the fibers that make me,
Lonely love is there and will not flee.

Surfacing only to let me not forget,
Lonely love stays put from the other I met.

Rooted in place and will never leave,
Still lonely love allows other love to be conceived.

# Love's Command

Universal energy comes from the heart's love when it is double,
Earthly infections never cause the two hearts any trouble.

Love's unity is charged by the double-heart's vibration,
While the reward of that love is heighten by human sensation.

Double-hearted love prolongs all human existence,
Guard double-hearted love for it defies all resistance.

# If It's Love 1 Cor. 13: 1-10

What if I were versed in all human language
And could interpret the tongues of angels
But didn't know how to speak words of love
I would only be vibrating noise for ears to hear
If I understood all the mysteries of the universe
And my wisdom surpasses that of Solomon
Without enough love to share with others
I would have nothing to give
If I possessed all the riches in the world
And stored them away from others
What would I gain if I didn't share
With my fellow man
Love is life's splendor that's never hoarded
And portioned at temperamental will
Love isn't kept at reachable length
But thrust without rational choice
Love can't keep score to remember evil
It rejoices in truth and forgiveness
With soothing strokes to humanities essence
While proclaiming self-honor as well as reverence
Love is an austere possessor
Yet gentle when distributed
It's never rude or boastful
But loyal to peace and harmony
Love can render selfishness
Yet self-sufficient and trusting
Love's nature is slow to anger
And void of jealousy
Love is giving to others
In spite of personal needs
Love shows no disrespect for differences
But embraces diversity with equality
Love wears the emblem of commonality
And never that of superiority
Love is sustained by grace
With homage and amazement to the grace giver
Love is the lifeline
That reaches beyond the unimaginable
And understands the unthinkable

That's portrayed by earth's masses
Love is the truest symbol of perfection
That causes all imperfection
To mislay power
What if I had that perfection?

# Everybody Got a Story

The never heard stories of life that's always untold,
Strategically stay tucked in the heart beyond age old.
Patterns are designed for all who lives,
And all of life pieces the designer gives.

The pieces of life that harbor what can't be told,
Is as meaningful as that which comes forth so bold.
The untold stories are here to stay,
The designer knew it would make us pray.

# Man's Boy

The evolution of the boy is now a man,
Flexing his muscles and claiming his stand.
Dreams of days to come are no longer denied,
The dreams come true with the Master by his side.

O' Universe hear the shifted rhythm of the heart,
Securing all thoughts that grants a manly start.
The visions of tomorrow are now today,
Acceptance of a man's reality the visions stay.

Yet the boy who is now a man,
Evolves only by the Master's plan.

# Counted Loss

The gain for the day can loose a lifetime soul,
Embracing the benefit of a loss restores life's control.

Dispiriting the importance of man's inborn greed,
Makes life's necessities no longer a need.

Dispelling the conjured notion of all earthly relief,
Leaves only a spirit filled mind to rest on heaven's belief.

Therefore, the gain of the day is found in the losses it portrays,
A day's true gain comes only when we pray.
Those are the gains that are never lost but here to stay.

# Life's Balance

The soul becomes obedient with a balance of fear,
Honoring the balance keeps all measure of safety near.

Improperly weighted on any side lessen a promised blessing,
A simple plea for balance is embedded in sincere confessing.

Too little fear is an abundance of an unbalance reality,
And too much fear causes life to distort all mentality.

Strive for the balance of fear,
It always draws the Savior so near.

# Reaction

God's powerful breath has been named the wind,
But it's just how He feels when we sin.
The direct rays of the sun are often called hot,
He is just upset about what we forgot.

When He shed tears and it's called rain,
He is deep in sorrow and washes away the pain.
Take heed from the sun's heat and the wind,
And gather thoughts that reframe from all sin.

Wipe your brow from God's sun-driven heat,
Knowing that His resurrection is complete.
Don't just cover from the heat and rain,
Reflect on the power of the Almighty's bloodstain.

# Life's Crossings

I crossed your path and you crossed mine,
The plan was not ours but that of the Divine.
Showing up where we were,
Confused us with an unmistakable blur.

But making the path twine into one,
Causes pleasure when we share the sun.
Staying on the same path was never a guarantee,
Sometimes it's life's crosses that make one flee.

Leaving behind the path that we crossed,
Makes the new paths appreciate what we lost.

# Weedin'

**Making way for betterment.  Up-rooting that which chokes the harvest.
Clearing the field with a joyful soul.**

*Evelyn Dilworth-Williams*

# For Certain

If my soul couldn't laugh
An emotionless stone
That never understood time's hand
A certainty of pain for all of man.

# Grace's Laughter

Laughter balances sorrow
To ensure a tolerable tomorrow
When the tears flood our face
An interpolation of laughter spirals grace
From heaven's door to our earthly space.

# Self-Laughter

Meaningless and annoying too
That's what a frown will do
Share what feels good to the soul
So just laugh at yourself
It will help you grow gently old.

*Evelyn Dilworth-Williams*

# Shared Laughter

Laughter cleanses cobwebs from the soul
The louder it gets my heart feels less cold
And spans my life into aged old
When shared laughter is often told.

# Laughing Now

The pain of the mind takes its toll
Still I'll search for laughter in my soul
Making use of it to manage life's folds
Which steers my mind back into control.

# Childish Laughter

Seek the laughter you used as a child,
Searching for it is needed for adult life-style,
Dig deep into the corners of your heart,
And each day will have a blissful start.

# Bedrock

**All that's of worth builds from a strongly influenced foundation.**

*Evelyn Dilworth-Williams*

# Never Forget: Echoes & Shadows

Hearing the echoes of a slave from my being
Stirs the reality of what life is still seeing
Jostling the slave into an isolated corner of my soul
And trying to enclose what's untamable and bold
Lets me hear a voice of deep earthly sorrow
Evoking the reality of all of earth's tomorrows
Sometimes I set my eyes on the shadow of a slave
That rouses a fear that I'll take to the grave
But it remains for all to see
The echoes and shadows are the slave's legacy to me
Incessantly reminding me of what could be
The slave's willpower securely walks with me
The slave's voice comes and talks with me
For the slave's being is there to ensure I stay free.

# BCNAA

The ones who want to know my name
I must go back to ones forcibly claimed
The commonality of their presence was color
Distinctly different from all of earth's others
The brilliancy of their melanin glistens in the sun
Which deflects sun rays like no other ones
Black Colored Negro African-American
Is the historical visibility of my facade
If still confused, just remember the dark clay
Made into the image of God.

A child of God...
Just call me a child of God.

# Rights

The truest civil rights of man
Stem from laws made from the highest plan.
It starts with the formation of the heart,
Guaranteed from the womb as we depart.

Not just a selected arrangement of seats on a bus,
And not given to some, but all of us.
There's a winning battle for each place on earth,
The victory was declared before the notion of birth.

When Sister Rosa sat on that bus,
She sat not alone but with all of us.
The outcome was where we placed our trust,
It was faith in time for mankind to be just.

# Real Integration

Racial integration
Makes for a strange relation
That mixes earth's congregation
To ne'er condemn discrimination
With no fear of recrimination
Thus, tolerance is obliteration.

# Anti-Poverty

Poverty, who said I was poor?
My pay day will come for sure.
My sun rose just like all others,
None risers didn't get paid another.
I'm still here receiving my pay day,
Observing poverty of life that didn't stay.
All that's given is for my presence,
For the riches of my breathing essence.

*Evelyn Dilworth-Williams*

# Africa's Child

Africa, Africa, you sit beyond sight on a far-off shore
You are foreign earth to your kin once known before
Yet my spirit harnesses the pounding of your pulse each day
And conjoins us no matter how distant or far away.

Africa, Africa, I feel your breath pass through my soul
Still an imaginary vision of you I rightfully behold
Africa, Africa, I am estranged without your presence
To be lessened by the likes of others of a different essence.

Africa, Africa, I await your arrival
And consciously cling to ways of human survival
I see mountains that are not my Kilimanjaro
I see rivers that are not my Nile
I see tree trunks that are not my Boa-Bab.

Yet the roots of my spirit are fixed on Mount Kilimanjaro
And also run deep beneath the trunk of the Boa-Bab
While strongly nestled into the bed of the Nile
So Africa, Africa, claim the presence of your stolen child.

# My America

America, America, I pledge my soul,
To ne'er forget the unwritten ancestral stories told.
You make for such worthy written decrees,
Only to embrace not all with human needs.

America, America, you have such a divisible heart,
But your statute discloses protection for all counterparts.
Justice from parchment is a frivolous feat,
For it's your indivisible heart I wish to meet.

America, America, there's such beauty in your words,
But beauty doesn't last, just 'cause it can be heard.
Capturing it must come from the heart,
Not the sounds of laws that is ne'er honored in the dark.

America, America, you are made by God,
To love and cherish with more than a facade.
A colorless liberty is needed in this great land,
For there is a sameness in blood for all of man.

America, America, your blend is of a rare face,
Melted into one, yet separated not by grace.
The majesty of your strength includes the mass,
Yet your bounty for many you cunningly pass.

America, America, you readily acknowledge my rights,
Still equality comes only when there are centuries of fights.
Pursuing happiness is undeniable, but few receive
Always in your said rights I do believe.

America, America, I still pledge my soul,
To ne'er forget the ancestral stories told.
No matter how long I vision shared control,
America in my heart's home you I will forever hold.

# Names

You called me nigger so I repeated it too,
Didn't know it meant I was less than you.

Often times called girl,
And I would smile because you acknowledge my presence,
Didn't know I was counted as livestock essence.

Sometimes I'd hear you call men folk boy,
Thought everything was all right 'cause they bowed with outward joy.

You used to say mammy to the matronly ladies,
And they would answer with respect and in a voice so polite,
Didn't know you'd forced your way in their daughter's beds at night.

You called all the older gentlemen uncle,
Never any of them were your kin,
All they needed was aged black skin.

Later colored became my new name,
For sure things had changed that would make us the same,
Only to realize nigger had been rearranged.

Then I became a nigra,
Especially when publicly addressed,
The feeling that time was near for me to be blessed.

Well there was the arrival of Negro,
You pronounced it quite well,
Your eyes I caught a glimpse and they resembled the bowels of hell.

Figuring by now I'd best name myself,
So I looked in the mirror, guess who stared back?
It was a face I called myself the color of Black.

With my name changing as often as it had in the past,
I knew being called Black was not going to last.

Needed something big and real,
Now I call myself a continent and a continent,

Makes for a good feeling to change my own name,
So whatever others call me I will no longer claim,
For I'm the only one who really hears my name.

# Believe

Communing with the past
Allows life's presence to last
With wise eyes in our head
Gives way to honor of the dead
Let there be a kindling of the spirit
Life yields are great so lets reveal it
Perceive not which is not yours
All is there on a distant shore
Vanity will always befall the beast
Show your sincerity even to the least
Minded minds reveal the needs
Its affect depends on your deeds
Pluck all that is of despair
It is yours alone to prepare
Wherefore there is nothing better
Than what God and man put together
Mind you the dust of the universe is scattered
All in tune will know what really mattered
So let your past not be forgotten
It's God's will to save the downtrodden
Rejoice in the present or the past
Future generations will need it to last
Believing makes us manifest as the whole
Forgetting not who is in control
Boundless preservation comes from within
Forget not your spirit the will to win
Supreme power guides us through barriers
Be a catalyst not just a carrier
A certainty a keeper of our beliefs
Lo the resurrection is our relief
Behold the presence of our past
Spirits of past endurance will forever last.

# Whispers from the Hull

Tossed to and fro with the sounds of a shackled voice,
Never grasping the reason for denial of choice.
While carried away by the winds of deception,
Quietly creating low harmonious sounds of protection.

In the hold chamber of dampness and darkness freedom disappears,
And a hush of sound is heard through muffled spirit ears.
The being of the captive not understood,
While unnoticeable survival sharing forms brotherhood.

The bond of unity is passed without sounds of commotion,
Perfecting survival with guarded gesture and quick motions.
The ebbing not of the eternal spirit is intact,
Even with doubtfulness of life's existence on their backs.

There is an inner whisper that soothes captivity's flaming sting,
And back to the motherland this sameness will bring.
The hopeful days of jubilee are sure to appear in time some more,
And you'll hear the whispers loudly return to the motherland's shore.

# Four Little Girls

The seeds of tarnished hate so ferociously sown,
Deeply rooted by the children of the worthless unknown.
Always faceless when making an appearance,
So they slithered along earth's path to sustain endurance.

The ole-tarnished seeds took four little girls from this earth,
Not because of any wrong, just their birth.
The faces of the little girls will appear again and again,
But the seeds of the unknown are not part of the Master's plan.

The first seats in hell are where the tarnished will be un-blest.
And the four little girls are with God's precious best.
Who the four little are we will always know,
Who they could have been, they never got a chance to show.

Yanked away by the hands of the tarnished from birth,
Forever remembered regardless of absence on this earth.

# Branded Gift Returned

Chained to the bondage holder's name,
And nothing of the native land is the same.
Just wearing the outward identity of the slavers,
But always enliven by the Savior.

Burning the claimant's emblem on my skin,
Enlarged the multitudes of their earthly sins.
Whereas the brands hottest fire is in the name,
Stripping identity of those forcibly claimed.

Disfigured by the stain of the assigned name,
Caused confusion and generational pain.
Destroyed kinship on the distant shore,
So take it back, it's not wanted anymore.

Just call me X: Tribute to Malcolm

# The Pink Hula-Hoop

Playing time is a child's daily concern,
Life begets the moment for a child to learn.
Twisting and shaking from head to toe,
Spreads enjoyment for a child to show.

A rise of fear comes when hooded hatred rides about,
But assured safety is in reach and playtime is not out.
The pink hula-hoop encased all that repelled any fear,
For there he was watching her as he stood so near.

While evil lurks dressed in clothing of hoods,
That imprint of playtime made life understood.
Her safety within the hula-hoop, colored pink,
Aborted what the hoods wanted her to think.

While playing, yet watching the expression on his face,
Made her vigilant of who could enter her heart's space.
Now to this day when man-made horror prowls about,
The pink hula-hoop and her Dad's expression shield it out.

# God Is...

One day I pretended to be white,
Dismissed people of color from my sight.
The day wore very much like it always had,
Separating from colors that made the world bad.

As night approached the ending of the day,
I decided to fall on my knees to bow and pray.
I searched the heavens and found no one to hear my say,
God had chosen to be colored on my chosen white day.

The next day I was my same black,
I too didn't want other races in my life's act.
As night approached the ending of my day,
I fell on my knees to bow and pray.

I searched the heavens and God heard my plea,
With a stern voice He said, "everyone is me,
My image is too big to be in one colored degree,
For I'm every color that human eyes can see."

# My Skin

Don't call me Black because of the color of my skin,
Call me Black from what my heart holds from within.
To know the feel of the chains of slavery's hold,
Causes me to be Black from the days of ancient old.

The belly of the vessels that shipped human cargo,
Created the color my heart wants you to know.
Just looking at my skin and swearing to identify me,
Unjustifiably marks me for there is more to see.

The tree limbs that my kin plummeted from when hanged,
Colors the Black skin that's beyond eyesight range.
Just to look at me and see a color,
Diminishes the gift of vision for another.

The deliberate degrading of my race,
Is what colors my Black face.
It's afar from what the eyes see when I appear,
But what the heart sends to the veneer.

Wearing the color of Black is a proud task,
Ne'er to be confused with my birthright's mask.
The color is pounded by the history of the blood,
And worn with honor and the beauty of a rose bud.

The awareness of my presence can never be called Black,
Centuries of hope deprivation keep my color intact.
Just a skin color is not who I claim,
My color has a heart-filled name.

My color is worn not by the outer skin,
But deep inside where my heart holds it within.
Black is the akin of my heart's ancestral kin,
Not what you see when you look at my skin.

# A Sixties Child

The clanking sounds of *toothbrushes on the back of the pews,
Made known to the world the children of the Sixties were not
through.
The last chain of humanity's time had to be snapped broken,
For generational bondage's word had to be loudly spoken.

Listening to the leaders of shared nonviolent tactics,
Caused pure imbedded madness to pierce a mind of peaceful antics.
Yet intensely listening whereas to know the importance to obey,
Bowing and kneeling was a demand as the leaders led us to pray.

Children of the Sixties prepared to mount,
For the day had come for all to give an account.
Ready to march, sing, and be seen,
Commanded the speaker of the "Dream."

Feet, hands, legs, eyes, and all other body parts,
Geared up to rearrange life's slave descendants start.
All was done with the mind in total control of the heart,
For the time was fated to recompense for ancestral counterparts.

The task of the water hoses and dogs was for the whole world to
view,
The Sixties children enacted the final legal round for freedom to
pursue.
The demands were of a very simple matter,
With hour zero left to be the world's latter.

Just one thought liberated each of our beings,
We wanted no more of our life seeing.
The choice to live or the choice to die,
The only human rights we wouldn't be denied.

Wanting free nothing, it was all about choice,
Rang from the children of the Sixties untamable voice.
The real volume of the revolution was not just to exist to survive,
Living in a land of enough opportunities for all, we too had to thrive.
Just Ask Me To Tell The Story …

* Symbolic of preparedness for jail

# Cottin Pickin' Freedom Riders

When Sister Rosa sat on that bus she didn't sit alone,
She had the visible image of the Master on the high throne.
There were passengers on that bus that no eye could see,
She was riding with people who had never been free.

Their time had come to sit and ride anywhere,
The day was now with no time to spare.
Cottin pickin' time had lasted for hundreds of years,
So taking a seat anywhere was done without fear.

Ridin' didn't quench the thirst of the workers of the fields
They needed more of what a water fountain could give
With their brow so hot none wanted to think,
God's fountains were sighted and used by them to drink.

Cottin by now was well learned,
That group wanted real schooling for degrees to earn.
Taking a desk at the schools of their choice,
Caused plenty ruckus from the established classes' voice.

They also had to find a way to get to the polls,
Directions to get there were not always told.
Pickin' a time to get to the polling place to vote,
Was with ease when unity was designed to promote.

The field hands by now had settled some claims,
There was much to do so they attracted some fame.
Saw water hoses used on the children of the cottin bedded south,
Started spreading the idea of boycotts by word of mouth.

People from everywhere caught a glimpse of their plan,
And the ridin' cottin pickers got support from all over the land.
They marched with placards until their feet were in pain,
Ne'er to stop for they knew that moment wouldn't come again.

Marching, walking, and singing got them put in jail,
Willingly they went not knowing who would post their bail.
Even when the newly found leaders gave of life,
They wouldn't relent just because of violent strife.

The job had to be done and the job was done,
Turning back was left for the total sum of none.
All that took place was not just for you or me,
But for the ones who were born and die not free.

*Evelyn Dilworth-Williams*

# Crown and Glory

My beauty is best shown with my natural hair,
Though others look with an estranged stare.
But it's my inborn state that I wish to share,
If I don't appreciate mine why should others care?

My hair reveals my true crown and glory,
And that's how I portray me in other's story.
Nature's simplicity bestowed on my being,
Is the offering I give for the world's seeing.

To reveal my trueness to the world,
I must wear my natural curl.
So I sport my hair in its best state,
Without the necessity to imitate.

My true beauty is in my gifts from God,
Not how I make-up the hair thing facade.
Therefore, I bring to the world my natural hair,
Adding to multiplicity of what's unique and rare.

# Crazy? ... Not!!!

Docility is what I sometimes choose to be.
Schizoid makes me feel deservingly free,
To handle the pain of being called nigger.
My reaction is naught; which makes me bigger.

Then again, I'm quick to get mad,
Diminishing a happy spirit into sad,
Predictability I still manage not to cling,
...Nigger, joy shows up, and "does its thing."

# Inheritance

The Emancipation Proclamation:
Sanctimonious stroke of legislation
A rearranged means to dominate
The design of that hollow mandate
Plus three slave amendments
Thwarted assurance of contentment
For those bearing a slave's face
Ne'er a bulwark for their race
Self-protection from this notion
Proclaimed generational commotion
Guarding the rearranged slave's face
Believing no legislation protects a race.

# Significant Past

Taking inventory of your existence's past
Assures the proper balance for the present to last
Noting all that renders measurable outcomes
Calculates life's totalities worth and worthless sums

Clearing all barriers that inhibits the growth of life's stay
While harnessing all that okayness needs to portray
Sifting away what shouldn't or can't be reclaimed
Life is forced to give what is yours, granted in your name

# Black-Blackness: Colored-Action

The color of my black-blackness,
Gleams from my inner soul's nowness,
Venturing to embrace life's trueness,
Masterfully striving to show oneness.
My blackness causes all my soul's being,
It's what the whole world is offered for seeing,
With candor that my hope will never exit fleeing,
My blackness is the imprisonment of my freeing.
Just how black is my blackness?
It's an ebony colored mind that nature created in black:
A non-exfoliating black that sticks with courage against designed odds.
A luminous black that makes opposite ends meet to see in the same direction.
A penetrating black that reaches deep to give one black hand to another.
A star-studded black with a lustrous sense of absolution when systemically aggrieved.
Where's the origin of my blackness?
The ancestral survival of the chains placed around the necks, arms and legs
of a slave mother
or a slave father
is of an intrepid blackness.
The generational maintaining of hope regardless of an assigned task
of breeding like livestock
is of a piercing blackness.
The inherited sustaining of the innate spirit as a child
is yanked from a mother's arms
for selling as a commodity
is of a saturated blackness.
The congenital endurance of human dignity
while standing on the auction block
with bids for one's being
is of a notorious blackness.
The inborn unbreakable mind
even when the oppressor
attempts to tame with lashes on their backs
is of an echoing blackness.

The hereditary nourishing of the human intellect
by pilfering an opportunity
to read at the cost of one's life
is of a prominent blackness.
Yet:
The blackness of my black is not what's visible to the naked eye
It is rooted into my true image, so deep no souls can deny.
It is my spirit's power that equates me to generational survival,
Never to be filtered as ordinary black by any of earth's revival.
The blackness of my black will forever protect my reason for being,
And future generational black will have true black-blackness for seeing.

# Whoze Dat Drawin Neer Me?

I'z stayz on m' knees
Did u knos dat Jezus ez 'n sum foak
I'mz down heer lookin fu Jezus
I'z heer de footsteps
Daze all kinds in dis sher wurl
But I'z not sho whoze da be
***Sho du hopes da be Jezus!***
Cuz no bodee lse w'du
I needze to git tu de Lawd
And Jesuz ez de onlee one tu sho de wa
***I'z sho du hopes u be Jezus!***
Effen u ain't hem dun git neer me
Cuz I'z needze to git tu de Lawd
De onlee way ez thru Hiz Son
And I knos dis and u knos dat tu
I heer de footsteps
***I'z sho du hopes da be Jezus!***
Hez ju didin die fu nutin
Hez didzit sos weed hav de gif uf eturnul life
And I'z sho nuf wun dat gif
I'z keeps uh heering de footsteps
***Sho du hopes da be Jezus!***
Fur Hez kin lite my path 'n life
Cuz hez de lite uf dis shere wurl
I knos dis and u knos dat tu
Datz y I hopes u be Jezus drawin neer me
Sum timez dose ole footstep I heer
Dunt be Jezus
And my soles jest leeps and run
Cuz nighn, I'mz jest gwine follo de footsteps uf His Sun
Iz sho du hope u be Jesuz drawin neer me
Fur itz de Savyuh I wonna cee
Soz m' sole kin be set free
Nign du uz undistan y I'z uh lizen on bendin knee
Fur dose footsteps drawin neer me
***Sho du hopes da be Jezus!***

# Jest Talkin Tu De Lawd

Lawdy, Lawdy, murcemebe,
I jest dun knos wha happ'em tu me.
I wuz jest sittin on de sho watchin' de sea.
When all uf a sudden' I'mz beggin and pleadin,
Fur my life on disshere one goud knee.
Lawdy, Lawdy, murcemebe.

Dun't da knos I'z wuz bone free?
Lawdy, Lawdy, murcemebe.
I'z jest lookin round bu I'z dun't undastan nutin I'z see
Crazed by the ne vu worz herred befo and no ansur tu my plea.
Dunt daz knos I'z tu wuz creeted by Thee?
Lawdy, Lawdy, murcemebe.

Yall I'z jest talkin tu de Lawd,
Hez gwine tu heh me, yall uh see!
Lawdy, Lawdy, murcemebe.
De Lawd gwine heh fum me!
Lawdy, Lawdy, murcemebe

*Evelyn Dilworth-Williams*

# Clearing New Ground

**Taking out the old remains to make for new growth.**

*Evelyn Dilworth-Williams*

# Today's Teen

I once was a teen,
I know what 13 to 19 means,
Though my hair is turning white,
What was wrong then is still not right.

The mysteries of all those long *ago(s),*
Are still what others are seeking to know,
Hearts of today feel pain the same way,
And abound with solace when they pray.

Youth is like a vapor or a faint mist,
With a propensity of several kinds of twist,
It's here today with such passionate vigor,
But dissipates with life's enormities to figure.

It's a commonality of maturation to be a teen,
For I once was like you I know what it means,
Hearing the voices of generations ahead,
Still is something that a teen daily dreads.

When the days of youth quickly fade,
And remembering how an adult is made,
Know that you are encircled by old teens,
And take advantage of what their life means.

I know this 'cause I once was 13 to 19,
And I'm mindful of what living life means.
Still I grow daily with my hopes and dreams,
While living life as though I'm still a teen.

# Lisee Luca

Sassy hairdos
And painted nails too
Changes the little girl
But it's still you.

A change is in your smile,
Still it transcends from your inner child.
You are the same from within,
It radiates just as it always has been.

Growing up is a natural evolution,
And soon life will depend on your own solutions.
But for now there is your family to depend,
To guide and protect you to the end.

Remember the truth of beauty comes from within,
And is marked on the outer skin.
Strong and good as a teen,
Makes way for what a real lady means.

Lisee Luca …
A blessing are you
Along with your sassy hairdos
and painted nails too.

# It's Okay

It's okay to differ from your friends,
When all about them is not your desired end.
Walk in the light of who you rely on and depend,
Choose your own reality not that of a friend.

It's okay to walk alone,
Especially when others are walking wrong.
You are protected from the High Throne.
When walking right as you walk alone.

It's okay to nurture your inner thoughts,
As others in sinful deeds are caught.
On Calvary the price was paid and bought,
So think your way; after all they are your thoughts.

It's okay to have your own beliefs
Tuning the Word heaven is your relief.
Comprising not of the world beneath,
Just being okay with your own beliefs.

To differ is okay,
As long as it is the Master's way.
Whether to a friend or to a foe,
Make known that you chart where you'll go.

# Dreaming Reality

A dream during the hour of daylight,
Makes for a pleasing ending in sight.
While the view is set plain,
Hopes of a dream are claimed.

Seeing exactness of measurable hope,
Sets into motion an attainable scope,
And reveals the mysteries of reality,
Ensuring dreams that realize finality.

The visibility of life beyond need,
Points the spirit to un-chartered deeds,
That amasses all and often without ease,
To live a life dreamed to please.

# Veracity

That which lies behind hopes and dream,
Are the things you claim and redeem.
The truth of hopes and dreams is reality,
Spun by your life's conscience vitality.

Hopes and dreams are for unseen success,
It's the starting point for unleashing your best.
Gazing passionately at hopes and dreams
Makes life's blueprint easier than it seems.

Hopes and dreams come not just in one size,
Your choice of either is what you can realize.
Reach high to never settle for I just don't know,
Hopes and dreams create what your life will show.

Embrace the seeds of your life's victory,
Ne'er bed it with those who are contradictory.
Hopes and dreams are for your personal sake,
A precious gift to procure for life's re-make.

# Glory nor Fame

To join the army for the spirit that's lame,
Tends not to get you earth's glory nor fame.
The eyes of the world turn and stare away,
Knowing well it is the spirit that will stay.

A healthy spirit has dominion over hell,
It fortifies the doors where Satan dwells.
Keeping out all those who attempt to ascend,
Controlling who stays and who gets in.

Worldly evil has been in charge too long,
Feeding on the innocent and luring them wrong.
The time to save the spirit is at hand,
A good spirit fits into the Master's plan.

Let us mount for the spirit to be free,
Then man will know what he was meant to be.
Fighting for the cause is not the wrong thing to do,
Lacking in the spirit finishes less than anew.

Preservation of the spirit is the fight's major goal,
Designed to recapture the Master's lost souls.
Life's outcome is best when the spirit is protected,
For man needs are cleansed by spirits not rejected.

# Life's Frown

Evilness wears such a deceiving custom,
And good is squiggly-wiggly just looking for room.
Evilness quickly gulps and consumes,
Yet good is forever lacking life's gloom.

The print of evil is shown all around.
Good embraces evilness without a sound.
Evilness devours with a lion's heart to control and bound,
But good always conquers and evilness spirals down.

# Recoup

Step up to the plate
it's your turn
Batter up and prepare
for the run
Time's out
for negligent fun
Mankind needs
a reclamation spun.

Maneuvering to instill
what's right
Is no doubt
the procreator's plight
Retreating for the lack of
remaining might
Taints the future image
in our natural sight

# Your Place

Sitting in this world on your tuff,
Thinking all about you ain't your stuff.
Oh, just wondin' how you'll do your best,
When all around you is just one big mess.

Pondering the whys of your space,
Just as those you love forget their place.
Amazed at the outcome of your life,
Yet lookin' the other way when there's strife.

Acknowledging the bigness of your situation,
But ne'er lifting a hand to stop its continuation.
Life just rollin' past you ever'day,
While never reaching out to bow to pray.

The ups and downs will always come and go,
So create a new place that will help you grow.

# Winner's Ticket

Life ain't no sweepstake child,
Chance didn't make you walk that extra mile.
Putting your hands on the plow,
Is just part of the why and the how.

Balancing life with working hard and steady
Lets you gird up your plan to get ready.
The real finish line is there for all,
So get in the game and stand tall.

Child, life just ain't no sweepstake,
Winning is for the ones who never self-fake.

# Or Designer's Makeup

I've got to put the right makeup on today,
Applying it where it will surely stay.
I'll use the top designer's products on my face,
Or shall I give thanks to Him for His loving grace?

I'm going to paint my lips a bright red,
Or let the Word pass from my lips to be said?
My cheeks need a touch of blush,
Or shall I touch someone who's low and crushed?

I've got to put the right makeup on today,
I need to apply the right amount where it will surely stay.
Before I do anything I need to put on a foundation that's just right,
Or shall I build a foundation that manifests in God's light?

I'm going to use a powder that is a perfect blend,
Or shall I set an example that opposes earthly sin?
I'll make certain that I don't forget to use a good lip liner,
Or perhaps I'll just portray the ways of life's true Designer.

I'll use my eyebrow pencil to give my eyes a perfect look,
Or shall I spend time with His instructional Book?
I've got to put the right makeup on today,
Or maybe I'll just stop and take time to pray.

Putting makeup on my face is all for the world to see,
But to make up my inner spirit is designed to please Thee.
Shall I only make up my face for my day to start?
Or shall I face today with a made up heart?

# Time Spent

Innocent time spent in the mist of earthly sin
Creates consciousness that's a troubling blend.
The yoke of seeing the days that are past,
Enrages the nowness of my soul to last.
The uneven gravity of long aged thoughts,
Makes innocent time void of fault.

# Words of Advice

Watch what you say it bears a resemblance of reality,
That attaches itself and become your finality.
Pace yourself with words that make strong belief,
For it might be your need for heaven's relief.
Orderly thoughts reveal tones that profitably manifest,
To set in motion a reality to give way to life's best.

# Jelly Meets Jam

So much alike that I'm afraid to say my name,
When you appear we all seem the same.
No point in actin' like you are better than me,
'Cause when in your space the same He'll see.

Our flavors give off such a similar taste,
Thinking our reality is made in confused haste.
Likeness makes it difficult for us to separate,
Thinking our self-defined difference is our fate.

Our uniqueness is not how we're made,
Time's toll makes us the same as we fade.
Embracing others with a life called a different name,
Assures us that a greater spirit made us all the same.

I don't know which I am,
Am I Jelly or am I Jam?
Well…
I'll try hard not to be who you are,
But who can tell whether close or afar?
Jelly meets Jam?
Or…
Jam meets Jelly?
I guess a power greater than us will tell-it.

# Dimples

A nonchalant look on the face of Dimples,
Impresses the thought that she is simple.
Sitting alone with only a half smile,
Others wonder if she's an adult or a child.

All about her makes sure she's fed,
And goes as far as to tuck her in bed.
Receiving the response of just a stare,
Others start planning for tomorrow's care.

Worn from a day of self-imposed demands,
Everybody's ready to throw up their hands.
While Dimple practices her nonchalant look plan,
To once again restart her day in total command.

# Self-Made

I am me because of me
Made perceptible for the whole world to see
Accrediting others with whom I surface to be
Renders impotence of my soul's plea
To always show me as spirit-free
To be or not to be
So I safeguard my destiny for me.

# Feathers or Spirits

Together we flock if our feathers are the same,
Still it's not the feathers the Master will claim.
The sightless sameness the spirit reveals,
All that's of worth the Master inwardly instills.

Together we flock if our inner spirits are the same,
For it's the spirits the Master will claim.
The liken spirit of heaven is what He wants revealed,
And heaven on earth is what the Master wants instilled.

A feather can blow in a feeble wind,
A spirit stays beyond life journey's end.
Feathers together have an expiration stay,
The spirits of life travel throughout time's way.

Birds of a feather or spirits together?
Should we flock because of our feathers
Or our inner spirits that bond us together?
Which will endure life's unruly weather?

# Schooling before School

When you go to school today keep your mouth closed,
Listen to the teacher and not to your buddies and those.
Get to class on time and stay in your seat,
If you don't understand ask your teacher to please repeat.
Be sure to carry your pencils, pens, and books to class,
Read and write with the teacher and what is learned will last.
While the teacher is teaching don't do a thing to upset the lesson plan,
For the teacher got an education long before your mischief began.
Don't stay at your locker too long and get to class late,
'Cause a good teacher will use that when it's time to evaluate.
Don't giggle, grin, or pass notes around the room,
When the teacher catches you—you'll surely be doomed.
If the lesson gets too hard and you don't understand,
Don't blurt out for help just raise your hand.
If your mind wonders on something not pertaining to the lesson,
Try hard to get back on track, for I'm praying for that blessing!
Now keep in mind why you are there,
'Cause lots of people love you and care.
Your schooling is important not only to you,
Because everybody wants to see you get through.
Know this; what you are doing is not just for you and me,
It's your show of appreciation of the divinity of Thee.
Don't forget to study hard while in school today,
No one will ever be able to take what you learn away.
So keep your mouth shut and pay close attention,
For if you don't, this lesson will surely again be mentioned.
Now go to school and do nothing less than your best,
You'll be successful, for the Master will do the rest.

# Heart's Harvest

**When all the work has been done, and nothing is left to do, just wait on the harvest to reap and put it away.  Life allows us to harvest what we plant, to store in the heart forever.**

*Evelyn Dilworth-Williams*

# The Heart's Harvest

Gathering goodness for the heart to keep,
Eases a daily walk for the soul to reap.
Tucking a ray of sunshine for a rain-filled day,
The heart will store it and there it will stay.
Selecting from the Master's harvest for the heart to reap,
Allows life to release what's stored in the heart to keep.

# Thanksgiving

Grace is the gift for thanksgiving,
Bound with mercy for all earth's living.
To receive the need to give honor for grace,
It is the daily task for the human race.

The yokes of life often appear without a hint,
But ease by an abundance of grace that's divinely sent.
The vision of faith grants stamina all so bold,
And the eyes of grace connect with the shepherd of the soul.

The grace of life constantly hinders no gift to man,
For such blessings are spread not by earthly hands.
The giving of thanks is the result of such a loving giver,
And the gift of grace is constantly delivered.

Thanksgiving is so plentiful as grace is so ample,
For the giver of grace is forever man's example.

# To Do

Starting a day like the morning dew
Softens my touch to all those in view
As the dew gently touches the blades of grass
So will I when meeting others as they pass.

# Still

Darkness appears to lessen what I see,
And I'm diminished with fear as can be,
Still the rising of the sun reassures me,
My life's walk is the promise from Thee,
For my shadow is your guarantee.

# Shadow

Emerging sunlight
Sets forth sight
Your presence I see
While walking next to me
Your power reflects my space
With your infinite gift of grace.

# Prayer

I'm all prayed up
With this trouble-filled cup
Never to wonder anymore
For life has tallied the score
I'm all prayed up
Seeking all kinds of relief
Beyond prayer is heaven's belief.

# My Blues

I've been sittin' here nourishing my moans all day long,
Listening to sad songs after song.
With a stream of cold tears and a bottle of hot beer,
I want to get up; for my spirit needs some cheer.
Just a sad song,
All day long.
This blues is my life misused.

# Limited

I know this,
Still I don't do it.
I acknowledge it,
Yet I don't believe it.
Who controls it,
Me or my choice?
I need a directive from your voice,
Come Lord, let me be your choice.

# Today

Yesterday
Didn't stay
For now is today
Existing as it may
Slowly becoming yesterday
Claiming thoughts to obey
Yesterday's medley becomes today.

# Yesterday's Value

Yesterday...
Went away
It's today
Existing as it may
Becoming another day
Claiming thoughts to portray
Harnessing parts to stay
Commanding one to obey.

# Just a Rainbow

The presence and gracefulness of the appearance of a rainbow,
Streaks the distant sky as one of the Master's gift to show.

Sudden attention is heavenly bound from all down below,
Ahhh! The Master got a gaze from all those He knows.

*Evelyn Dilworth-Williams*

# An Instance

The seed of a wildflower
Grows with a divine shower
Blooming at its own pace
Challenging the human race.

Void of man's nourishment
Springing forth encouragement
For the blossom is brilliantly grand
Still no stroke from a mortal hand.

# Shared Parts

The fullness of the earth is of no claim,
Surely to be shared by all the same.

Gathering of some and sorting of pieces,
Makes way for the Creator's selected releases.

No man happily owns any staked parts,
The earth belongs to the Creator of its start.

# A Still Moment

The misty morning of stillness appeared without a warning
Knowing not the need of humanity's discerning
And calmness was laced with an unearthly hold
Streaking so quickly that consciousness was never told
Yet a chilling glimpse of awareness appeared
While a momentary surge of heavenly blessing was drawn near
The misty morning staked her claim on someone so dear.

# Life's Glow

The rising of the sun appears each day,
And sets with a daily command it must obey.
The rays strike the surface with a glow so bright,
Then slowly slants and all to see is the night.
Thoughts of the mind gather throughout its stay,
Never enough thought to claim ownership of the day.

# Eden

Temptation is part of life's design
Rooted into Eden's ground
Yielding is a choice for all mankind
Budding wherever humanity is found.

Temptation is life's reality
Limitless to the claims of man
Its enormity exceeds all mentality
God halts temptation: even on Eden's land
Still the choice to choose will eternally stand.

# Autumn Leaves

Discerning the unchangeable,
When summer leaves for autumn,
And knowing the certainty of winter,
Clinging to nowness of life's offerings.
While the mind shortens its mentality,
And the statue changes its vitality,
Knowing that's to come is reality,
Still autumn leaves.

# About The Author

Evelyn Dilworth-William is a secondary teacher, guidance counselor, and a master facilitator of parenting education. She received her B.A. in Sociology from Miles College in Fairfield, Alabama. She is also a graduate of the University of Alabama in Birmingham Graduate School of Education in Guidance and Counseling, with additional study in Family Counseling. She is also a certified parenting facilitator by Active Parenting Publishers of Atlanta, Georgia. Dilworth-Williams enjoys writing as well as reading poetry. Some of her most recent readings of her poetry have been at the Civil Rights Institute in Birmingham, the public library in Birmingham, various heritage affairs, and social gatherings. Her poetry is one of the counseling techniques used with her students and their parents. Her poems range from inspirational to down right humorous. Dilworth-Williams poetic motivation is a blend of all life's energy.

www.ingramcontent.com/pod-product-compliance
Lightning Source LLC
Chambersburg PA
CBHW051427280526
45785CB00003B/1190